UNITED STATES

By Jennifer Lombardo and
Sharon Gordon

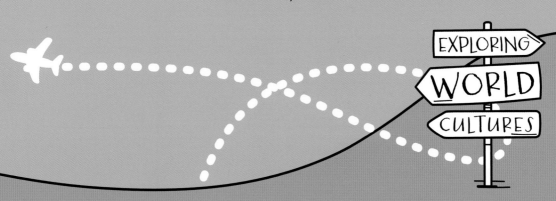

EXPLORING
WORLD
CULTURES

Cavendish
Square

Published in 2023 by Cavendish Square Publishing, LLC
2544 Clinton Street, Buffalo, NY 14224

Library of Congress Cataloging-in-Publication Data

Names: Gordon, Sharon, author. | Lombardo, Jennifer, author.
Title: United States / by Sharon Gordon and Jennifer Lombardo.
Description: [Second edition] | Buffalo, NY : Cavendish Square Publishing,
   [2023] | Series: Exploring world cultures | Includes index.
Identifiers: LCCN 2022033000 | ISBN 9781502667144 (library binding) | ISBN
   9781502667137 (paperback) | ISBN 9781502667151 (ebook)
Subjects: LCSH: United States--Juvenile literature.
Classification: LCC E156 .G673 2023 | DDC 973--dc23/eng/20220712
LC record available at https://lccn.loc.gov/2022033000

Writers: Sharon Gordon; Jennifer Lombardo (second edition)
Editor: Jennifer Lombardo
Copyeditor: Shannon Harts
Designer: Andrea Davison-Bartolotta

Find us on

CONTENTS

INTRODUCTION

In 2021, a **poll** of more than 20,000 people worldwide named the United States of America as the most powerful country in the world. However, with great power comes great **responsibility**. Many Americans and others around the world believe the United States has a responsibility to work with other countries to deal with big problems such as **climate change**.

I WANT YOU
FOR U.S. ARMY
NEAREST RECRUITING STATION

This character is "Uncle Sam"–a nickname for the United States.

Many people in the United States have good lives. They can afford a home, food, and health care. However, many other people cannot. Poor people often have trouble getting help for their basic needs. Although the laws say everyone is equal, some people are not always treated equally in the United States. This includes women, People of Color, **LGBTQ+** people, and people who are not part of the Christian faith. Many Americans love their country and want it to be the best it can be, so they are working to fix these problems.

The United States works on problems with other countries as part of the United Nations.

GEOGRAPHY

The United States is a large country. This is true of how much land there is as well as how many people there are. The country is separated into 50 states. The United States also has 14 territories.

This rock formation, called The Wave, lies between the states of Arizona and Utah.

The United States is bordered by Canada to the north, Mexico to the south, the Pacific Ocean to the west, and the Atlantic Ocean to the east. Northern states usually have longer winters and short, mild summers. Southern states are warm most of the year. Climate change is affecting these seasons, though.

Because of its size, the United States has a lot of **diversity** in plant and animal life. For example, giant redwood trees grow in the states of California and Oregon, while cacti are found in the Southwest.

PUERTO RICO

Puerto Rico is the most populated U.S. territory. In 2020, a poll found that 52 percent of Puerto Ricans want it to be the 51st state.

HISTORY

The country that is now the United States started off as 13 colonies. The people who lived in those colonies were ruled by Great Britain. They won the war for their independence in 1783. Over time, the government added new lands to the new country.

This map shows which countries the United States got its land from.

From 1861 to 1865, the Northern and Southern states fought the American Civil War because the Southern states wanted to keep Black people enslaved. The North won, and the government made slavery illegal. However, **racism** is still a big problem in the United States.

Beginning around 1900, the United States began to be seen as a world power. Americans have fought in wars around the world, including World War I (1914–1918) and World War II (1939–1945).

THE TRAIL OF TEARS
Between 1837 and 1839, the United States government forced the Cherokee, Choctaw, Chickasaw, Creek, and Seminole peoples to leave their homes on a death march called the Trail of Tears.

*Many different Native American **cultures** lived in what is now the United States long before the Europeans arrived.*

GOVERNMENT

The United States has a form of government called a democracy. This means people elect their leaders to make laws based on what the people want.
Each part of the government is described in the country's **constitution**, which was written in 1787.

The president lives in the White House.

The government is separated into three parts, or branches. The legislative branch is called Congress. It is made up of the House of Representatives and the Senate. Congress writes new laws and votes on which laws to pass. The judicial branch is made up of the courts. The executive branch makes sure people follow the law. It includes the president, vice president, and the Cabinet. The Cabinet is a group of people the president appoints to give him or her advice.

AN IMPORTANT PAPER

The Constitution is very important to many Americans. However, one poll found that about 41 percent of Americans believe it is out of date and should be rewritten.

Congress meets in the U.S. Capitol building in Washington, D.C.

THE ECONOMY

The United States has the largest **economy** in the world. It exports, or sends out, items such as gasoline, cars, and computer parts. It imports, or brings in, items such as computers, medicine, and oil.

Because of its large economy, the United States is a very rich country. However, there is a huge gap between the richest and poorest people. Many people have a hard time paying for important things such as food, clothing, and visits to the doctor. It can be very hard for poor people to get help. The jobs that are easy to get often do not pay enough for people to live on. Some people living in the United States have two or three jobs but are still poor.

FACT!
The United States spends more money on its military than any other country worldwide.

HARD WORKERS

Americans value hard work. They work in a wide variety of jobs, including farming, working in factories, teaching, health care, and business.

The most common job in the United States is **cashier**.

More than 500,000 Americans are homeless. Some sleep in tents on city streets.

THE ENVIRONMENT

The United States has played a big role in creating climate change. Some states have started trying to fix this problem. They are switching to clean energy, such as wind and solar power, that does not worsen climate change as much as using oil and gas for energy. However, many parts of the United States still depend on oil and gas. Digging in the ground for these **resources** is bad for the environment, or natural world.

FACT!

The oldest trees in the world are 5,000-year-old bristlecone pines in Nevada, California, and Utah.

National parks such as Zion are set up to keep nature safe.

Plastic pollution is another problem. Americans use a lot of plastic bags, straws, and other items. When these are not thrown away or recycled properly, they often end up in the environment. Animals can get hurt or die because of this garbage. Many Americans are trying to use less plastic in their daily lives.

Many Americans asked the government to prevent the building of a huge new oil pipeline, the Keystone XL, in 2011.

GOVERNMENT HELP

The Environmental Protection Agency (EPA) passes laws to help keep the air, water, and soil safe for Americans.

THE PEOPLE TODAY

The United States is often called a country of **immigrants**. Everyone who lives in the country except for Native Americans came from somewhere else at one time or another. Today, more people immigrate to the United States than to any other country in the world.

As of 2020, about 60 percent of Americans were white, 19 percent were Latine, 13 percent were Black, 6 percent were Asian, and 1 percent were Native American. Almost 3 percent were a mix of two or more races.

The United States has a lot of diversity.

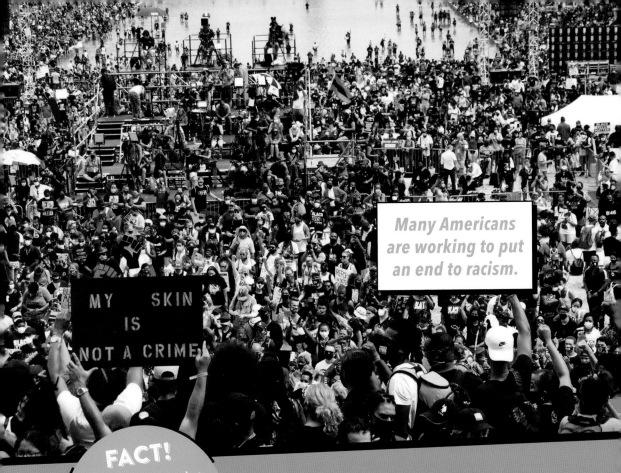

Many Americans are working to put an end to racism.

MY SKIN IS NOT A CRIME

CITY LOVERS

Most Americans—83 percent—live in cities. About 40 percent live on the East Coast, and about 16 percent live on the West Coast.

Immigrants often deal with **prejudice** and racism from people who were born in the United States. However, many immigrants are willing to take this risk because they are running away from war or other dangers in their home country.

17

LIFESTYLE

The lifestyle of an American living in New York City is very different than that of someone who lives on a farm in Montana. Additionally, the country is so large and so many immigrants have made their home there that it is hard to talk about what a "normal" American lifestyle is. This depends a lot on things, such as a person's faith, location, and beliefs about the government.

Americans like to spend time with friends, and eating out is a popular way to do this.

In general, Americans are outgoing and willing to share their opinions. They often value **politeness**, but this looks different in different areas. For example, in the Northeast, it is polite not to waste someone's time by talking too much. In the South, it is polite to stop and chat with people.

AMERICAN INGENUITY

Many Americans value ingenuity, or inventiveness. They are proud of other Americans who think of creative ways to solve problems.

There are many small towns as well as big cities in the United States.

RELIGION

The United States has no official religion, or faith. The Constitution says people are free to practice any religion they want—or none at all. However, some people believe the country should follow Christian ideas about what is right and wrong. In everyday life, some Americans are not accepting of other religions. For example, Muslims—people who practice Islam—are sometimes treated poorly because of their religion.

There are almost 3,000 mosques, or Muslim prayer houses, in the United States.

CHRISTIAN BEGINNINGS

Christians called Puritans were some of the first Europeans to come to North America. Their ideas still affect American culture today.

Most Americans are Christian, and most American Christians belong to a sect, or group, called Protestantism. However, almost every religion in the world is practiced somewhere in the country. These include Judaism, Hinduism, Sikhism, and Buddhism. About 23 percent of Americans say they have no religion.

Christmas is a major holiday in the United States even for some non-Christians.

LANGUAGE

The United States does not have an official language. Most people speak English, but as many as 430 other languages are spoken. Many people, especially immigrants, speak more than one. Other commonly spoken languages include Spanish, French, Chinese, Vietnamese, and Cherokee. School is taught mostly in English. About 20 percent of students learn a second language. Spanish and French are the most commonly taught.

This item is called a shopping cart, carriage, or buggy in different parts of the United States.

English sounds different from one place to another. People have different ways of saying the same thing. People from the South might say, "Hey, y'all," instead of "Hello, everyone." Some people call soft drinks "soda," and others call them "pop." In the South, all soft drinks are often called "Coke," no matter what the brand is.

Many words and place names, including "skunk," "squash," "Massachusetts," and "Wyoming," come from Native American languages.

A COMMON LANGUAGE

The third most common language in the United States is American Sign Language (ASL).

ARTS AND FESTIVALS

There are thousands of festivals, or special gatherings, held every year in the United States. These include art festivals, music festivals, flower festivals, food festivals, and many more. Concerts are very popular in the United States. Many people travel to other states to see their favorite musicians in person. American music, movies, and books are popular in many other countries.

Jazz is a type of music that was created by Black communities in New Orleans, Louisiana.

Unlike many other countries, the United States does not have one **traditional** or easily recognizable style of artwork or music. However, many Native American cultures do have traditional art styles. In addition, from the 1910s to the mid-1930s, artists from the mostly-Black neighborhood of Harlem in New York City became very popular. In the 1940s, Norman Rockwell created famous paintings of everyday American life.

Totem poles are traditional art made by western Native American groups such as the Tlingit and Haida.

POP ART

Andy Warhol was an American artist who became famous for his unusual art style. In 1961, he invented "pop art," or paintings of store-bought products.

FUN AND PLAY

Americans like to do a lot of different things for fun. Playing and watching sports are two popular activities. Soccer (football in most other countries), baseball, basketball, and American football are the most-watched sports. People also enjoy going shopping, making crafts, watching movies, and reading books. Outdoor activities such as rock climbing, hiking, and boating are common in nice weather. Parades are held on many holidays, such as the Fourth of July and Thanksgiving.

The United States has many beautiful hiking trails.

One very American activity is gun collecting. Many Americans enjoy owning different kinds of guns and going to special areas called shooting ranges to safely shoot at targets. However, not everyone in the United States uses guns in a safe way. This is why many Americans believe there should be stronger laws about who can have and use a gun.

Americans often invite friends over to watch TV together.

TV FOR FUN

Americans watch about four and a half hours of TV per day. That is more than any other country in the world.

FOOD

As immigrants came to the United States, they brought food from their home countries with them. Over time, these dishes were often "Americanized," or made differently in the United States.

A NATIVE AMERICAN FOOD

The Navajo created frybread when the United States government forced them to leave their homes. Today, many Native Americans consider this food part of their culture.

Barbecue is popular all year round, but it is especially common at summer picnics.

Burritos, pizza, egg rolls, and many other foods were either created or changed by Americans. In many cities, people can buy food that is made more like it is in other countries. Greek, Italian, Chinese, and Mexican are all popular food styles. At picnics in the summer, many families grill hot dogs and hamburgers. Ice cream and cake are typically served at birthday parties.

Enslaved people had a huge **influence** on many parts of American culture, including food. They brought plants such as watermelon, okra, and black-eyed peas with them from Africa.

FACT!
Americans eat more than 10 billion doughnuts every year.

More fast food is eaten in the United States than in any other country.

GLOSSARY

cashier: A person who is responsible for giving out or taking in money at a store.

climate change: Long-term change in Earth's weather, caused mainly by human activities.

constitution: A document that describes the laws of a country.

culture: The beliefs and ways of life of a group of people.

diversity: The quality or state of having many different types, forms, or ideas.

economy: The process or system by which goods and services are made and sold in a country.

immigrant: A person who comes to another country to live.

influence: The act or power of causing an effect or change without use of direct force or authority.

LGBTQ+: Relating to a group made up of people who see themselves as a gender different from the sex they were assigned at birth and people who are or want to be in relationships that aren't only male-female. LGBTQ stands for lesbian, gay, bisexual, transgender, and queer or questioning.

photography: The process of taking pictures with a camera.

politeness: The act of showing courtesy or good manners.

poll: To question in order to get information or opinions about something, or the question itself.

prejudice: A feeling of unfair dislike directed against an individual or a group because of some characteristic (such as race or religion).

racism: The practice of treating others poorly because they are part of a different race, or group of people who look alike in certain ways.

resource: A usable supply of something.

responsibility: Something a person must take care of or be in charge of.

traditional: Following what's been done for a long time.

FIND OUT MORE

Books

Dunbar-Ortiz, Roxanne, Jean Mendoza, and Debbie Reese. *An Indigenous Peoples' History of the United States for Young People*. Boston, MA: Beacon Press, 2019.

Langholtz, Gabrielle, Jenny Bowers, and DL Acken. *United Tastes of America*. New York, NY: Phaidon, 2019.

Website

National Geographic Kids: United States
kids.nationalgeographic.com/geography/countries/article/ united-states
Learn more about the United States here.

Video

Kids Meet a Native American Politician
www.youtube.com/watch?v=iY6ElwJxrcE
Kids ask a Yakama man named Asa questions about his culture.

INDEX